How to
Kingdom and Business
The Most Excellent Way

Phil Hanson

Terry Young

GROVE BOOKS LIMITED
RIDLEY HALL RD CAMBRIDGE CB3 9HU

Contents

Acknowledgments

The authors would like to express thanks to the many working colleagues who have unwittingly contributed to this piece of work simply by their actions and behaviour in real-life situations. We would particularly like to acknowledge the Faith in Business network, led by Richard Higginson and Peter Heslam, through which this collaboration came about. They also wish to thank those who provided the material for the Case Studies and permission to write them up and publish them: Simon Macauley, Jerry Marshall, Matt and Dr Sam Parfitt, and Peter Riley. In addition, there is a much wider community of interested parties whose observations and conversations continue to shape the thoughts shared in this booklet. It would be remiss not to acknowledge our families for their grace in letting us spend so much time in shaping and sharing these ideas and outputs.

First Impression January 2024
ISSN 1470-854X
ISBN 978 1 78827 363 3

1

What's the Problem?

This booklet describes a piece of work that started as a joint reflection of the two authors looking back over their working lives, each writer drawing on experiences of science, engineering and business leadership as well as Christian mission and ministry.

Over a period of two years, through weekly dialogue, each of the ideas offered here has been discussed between the authors, shared with an international network of peers, and the results have been published and reviewed in blogs and journals. In this booklet this work is consolidated and offered for wider debate and experiment.

We, the authors, have been hugely encouraged by the growing focus on Christians at work and the burgeoning Christian or kingdom business scene, not to mention the global network of Christian investors.

We each, however, had niggling worries about how anyone could know how much good was being done by business. Businesses cannot help changing the world and may be a force for good and bad at the same time. The question that had not been addressed to our satisfaction was how to measure the degree to which any business does or does not live up to kingdom values.

There is lots of help out there to encourage people to be better Christians at work, but very little on how their ethical impact might diffuse into the wider system. This is a question for startups, for entrepreneurs, for existing businesses and business subgroups, as well as for investors. There are principles here that may also help Christians in any workplace: whether company, charity or church.

What is Different?

We are not the first to walk these paths and we acknowledge the impact of many others in this field.

In this project, the idea of 'kingdom,' when used adjectivally and applied to business, indicates that whilst we may not be able to offer a soundbite definition of the destination we can acknowledge a direction of travel. We can work out what is and what is not kingdom.

In this work we are building a bridge that spans the worlds of faith and business. That bridge is built on solid, well-defined plinths on each side. The apostle Paul's framework of faith, hope and love underpins the faith pillar. Well-known models of business excellence underpin the business pillar. The result is an approach that enables us to give equal authority and weight to what we know about both faith and business. We are primarily looking at business through a critical faith lens, but the opposite perspective also works.

Why Read On?

This booklet is for those who first identify with the idea that, over and above individual Christian witness and example, a business may also make a positive difference in the world by following a kingdom direction. Secondly, it is for those who have a curiosity about how to measure company progress in that journey.

The goal of this work is to advance practical tools for business leaders. On the belief that the more people involved, the better will be the design, there is an implicit invitation to the reader to join us in this aim.

Business as Mission and Ministry

2

> Now we must find an approach to economic justice that works in fair weather and foul, but that will require brilliance, vision and political leadership. Another Keynes is needed. It is only within such a global system that it is possible for individuals, businesses and societies to dethrone Mammon, and to give all for the pearl of great price.
>
> *Archbishop Justin Welby*[1]

There has long been a debate about whether there can be such a thing as a Christian business. Does a business that is led by a Christian somehow automatically become a Christian business, for example? How is an ethical business different from a Christian business? Is there an opportunity for business leaders that is an 'octave' above personal witness (here, we use octave in the sense of playing the same notes but breaking through more clearly)?

In his second letter, Peter urges us 'to look forward to the day of the Lord and to hasten its coming' (2 Pet 3.11–12a). It is this idea of advancing the kingdom through our actions that prompts us to explore businesses that do just that.

There have been times when the idea of Christian business would have been much less confusing. Monasteries, for example, have always been places for both work and prayer, with daily patterns to ensure that neither of these purposes overtook the other. The Victorian philanthropists represent another chapter in history in which faith and business have been similarly integrated. George Cadbury's biographer, for example, paints a picture of a man who saw business and politics as instruments of service for religion.[2] He believed that environment made a difference to employees' well-being and was passionate about gardens for children. He also set a strong example in matters of keeping fit, while his commitment to education lasted a lifetime, including teaching at the adult institutes he himself had established – the rehabilitation centres of their day, and an alternative to the public house.

All this helps to identify two directions of travel for any company. The first strives for ever-improving efficiency and effectiveness. Through best practice companies boost operational performance, customer satisfaction and market share. The second direction is values-based and allows them intentionally to pursue virtue.

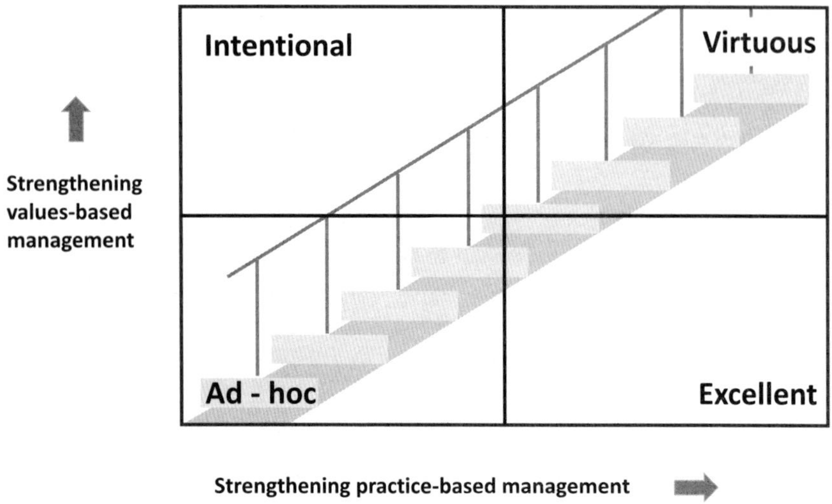

Reality, of course, is not as neat as this since every code of practice reflects some ethic. But this simplification allows us to address beliefs and practices separately. This booklet appeals to Christian ethics that seek first God's kingdom, but the reader may invoke their preferred ethic, sacred or secular.

Jim Collins' well-known book, *Good to Great*, explores the difference between ordinary well-run businesses and those few that achieve extraordinary success.[3] Kingdom business might be described as *great to goodness*, where excellent businesses make a real and positive difference in the world.

In finding ways to measure progress, the approach in this work is to ground assessment securely in both directions, building on well-attested best practice guides for business excellence and on the triplet of virtues—faith, hope and love—for ethical behaviour.

Although it may not always be onward and upward, the staircase metaphor in the figure shows how both journeys must combine to sustain a company's kingdom ambitions. This mirrors the idea of small steps of personal faith being rewarded with understanding. As Anselm said, 'I believe so that I may understand.'[4]

Turning to the four quadrants, a broad basis for classification emerges:

Ad-hoc Businesses

Ad-hoc businesses do what they can and may well rely on the goodwill or enterprise of their employees to make them work. Management does its best and tends to get through in the end.

Excellent Businesses

Excellent businesses work systematically to improve their operations and workforce management, their engagement with clients and suppliers and their ability to execute strategic plans.

Intentional Companies

Intentional companies are often set up for the greater good, rather than profit margins. When the virtuous goals outweigh other considerations, such companies are anchored in the top left-hand quadrant.

The Virtuous Ideal

Finally, there is a virtuous ideal, that fully reflects ethical aims and delivers them through a finely-tuned business engine.

An intentional business will still need to embrace operational best practice if it is to survive in the long term, while an excellent business needs to become as systematic about its pursuit of virtue as it is about its pursuit of excellence, if both are to become truly virtuous.

This raises questions around what trajectory works best, and from which starting point. First, can *ad-hoc*, intentional and excellent businesses all transition with equal ease to the virtuous—for us, that is, the kingdom—quadrant, or will one need to take a step back? Clearly one size does not fit all, so instead this booklet provides the tools to help you measure where you really are when you start out and the progress you are making once you embark on the journey.

However, there is also the question of slippage (which has proved incredibly difficult for many organizations to resist). While many businesses trace their origins to Christian founders, most have experienced a creeping trajectory towards greater secularization, in which they slip back down the vertical axis. This is also true in the charity sector, where non-Christian governance has sometimes gradually eroded an original Christian calling.

The idea that good business should do good is not the exclusive preserve of faith-based initiatives. There are increasing numbers of business leaders who recognize that their activities can and should be a genuine platform for making the world a better place. Secular networks like B Corp[5] and Business in the Community[6] offer encouragement and practical support to businesspeople who wish to be socially responsible. Widely-used templates of business excellence (The USA Malcolm Baldrige Award[7] and the European EFQM[8] model (for example) go some way to suggesting that business best practice inherently demands a high degree of social responsibility. That said, even the best run businesses still have ethical blind spots.

One challenge is that humans have spoiled God's picture of work—a topic picked up in chapter three. To understand the X factor that differentiates kingdom businesses from excellent secular or ethical business it is necessary to find a critical kingdom lens through which to examine business enterprises, which is what chapter four is all about. Having done that, measuring where you are and where you want to go is the final step; methods for doing so are presented in chapter five.

Summary

- Searching for a kingdom ideal is one way to engage with Peter's call to work towards the coming of the day of the Lord (2 Pet 3.11–12a).
- The 2x2 *Staircase* matrix is presented in which the pursuit of virtue parallels the more usual pursuit of business excellence.
- This matrix provides a means of classifying companies—*ad hoc*, excellent, the virtuous ideal and intentional—and a basis for planning progress.

Case Study—Green Pastures CBS[9]

This example highlights several features around harnessing Christian intent to good business practice. Green Pastures is at one level a successful property company with all the associated competencies. It operates as a competitive business in the real world. However, its Christian origins and overriding aim of eradicating homelessness clearly differentiates it. Financial sustainability goes hand in hand with achieving its mission. Its kingdom reach is greatly multiplied through its network of church and charity partnerships and its vision goes beyond housing to the full rehabilitation of tenants into the world of work and self-sufficiency. It makes no secret of its overtly Christian purpose.

Pastor Pete Cunningham grew up in London, found faith at the age of 21 after being a somewhat riotous teenager and started working in the stock market. In 1993 he took on a small congregation in Southport, now Shoreline Church. He has always had a heart for the broken and homeless, feeding them and providing shelter where possible, even once in a caravan on the church car park. Inspired by the story of the Good Samaritan and gently sceptical about local authority initiatives, he and the other church leaders stepped out in faith when a desperate young family came along in 1999. Pete cashed in his pension plan and, with his son Andrew and co-director Vicki Woodley, purchased two flats for cash. Green Pastures Housing was born. By 2006, there was a bed for every person in need in Southport: they had ended the town's rough sleeping crisis. In 2010 Green Pastures opened a Community Benefit Society with charity status, allowing it to issue unsecured loan stock. Interestingly, it also allows investors to choose their rate of interest up to a maximum of 5%. Some non-investors simply make donations, but this represents a tiny percentage of the total income. At the time of writing, it has received more than £47 million in total investment. As a social enterprise, Green Pastures reinvests all its financial surplus to support its core mission of housing and supporting those facing homelessness.

As authors we identify this as a kingdom business because of the combination of Christian intent and operational effectiveness. Now operating nationally, the overall business vision is to 'End Homelessness.' Using its architecture and development skills Green Pastures also undertakes commercial building projects, often for churches, where again the profits go back into the homeless housing core business. Each new housing project is aligned with a partner church or charity which takes responsibility for pastoral care for the tenants.

Today, alongside Green Pasture's Direct projects there are over 90 such partners collectively housing more than 1,500 people. In 2023 the aim is to house 225 more people. Green Pastures also invest in other social enterprises, particularly to help partners get started, purchase materials, or with training. There is a heart to see residents enabled to re-enter the world of work. At the Mattersey Hall Training Centre, for instance, men and women are trained and equipped with key skills and encouraged in spiritual development. The programme provides a way out for those whose opportunities have been restricted by their social circumstances, family upbringing, physical problems, educational shortfalls and even their own poor choices. Partner organizations are asked to report regularly on 'kingdom performance indicators' that build an overall picture of the difference being made to people's lives and faith journeys.

3 Redeeming Work and Business

> Capitalism is nothing more than the result of countless individual and corporate decisions, and for good or ill, the capitalism we have is the capitalism we have chosen; its redemption rests on the choices we are yet to make.
>
> Kenneth Barnes[10]

The term 'invisible hand' first appeared in Adam Smith's work, *The Wealth of Nations*.[11] It is a metaphor for how, in a free market economy, self-interested individuals operate through a system of mutual interdependence, which encourages producers to make what is socially necessary, even though they ultimately care only about their own interest. Unfortunately, the invisible hand does not always produce socially beneficial outcomes, and can encourage greed, inequalities and other harms.

Ken Barnes argues that there is a moral vacuum at the core of capitalism that gets filled by the values of those who can impose them.

As noted, Christians have stepped up and shaped the workplace in line with their ethical outlook at times. For instance, Victorian, mainly nonconformist, pioneers introduced pensions, affordable housing and workers' recreation in a spirit of ethical adventure. In doing so, they provided an alternative to the despotic mills where Marx and Engels saw only seeds of revolution.

Spoiling the Job

Not only does business not have an ethic of its own, but good beginnings are not very 'sticky' and generally fade within a generation. The apostle Paul reminds us of the worst that is in us, which is often what fills the vacuum in Gal 5.19–21: 'sexual immorality, impurity and debauchery; idolatry and witchcraft; hatred, discord, jealousy, fits of rage, selfish ambition, dissensions, factions and envy; drunkenness, orgies, and the like.' Sadly, this behaviour can be seen as frequently in today's workplace as in the wider culture.

As we write, the Confederation of British Industry is being rocked by a sex scandal. Elsewhere, journalist Emily Chang reports on the workplace culture of Silicon Valley with eyewitness and anecdotal evidence of sexual harassment, online trolling and sex parties as part of a culture that connects sex to success.[12] Nearer to home, helplines for sexual harassment at work and guidance for employers speaks to a rising tide. Without labouring the point, unwanted advances are too much a part of working life, both painful in the moment and in the aftermath.

Let us take another characteristic from that list: how close have you come to idolizing your job, its status, pension, share options and opportunities to travel? How about the images of success at work, the ones that may be hanging on the office wall? Have you ever felt bereaved when you lost a job? It is not difficult for any of us to join the dots in Paul's list—perhaps linking idols to selfish ambition, or the loss of self-control when something gets in the way.

The connection with witchcraft as found in those verses from Galatians might puzzle Western readers. But let us remember that there are parts of the world where the need to keep the spirits onside, or perform occult practice, are more visible. In any case, there is plenty of online advice about how to make the most of your star sign in business.

From this wider perspective, the question is what is driving decisions and shaping the workplace culture?

Fixing the Workplace

The tendency for business to be manipulated by the few against the many has long been recognized. Here we look at three drivers of change, before we turn to the thornier problem of how to redeem the workplace rather than simply ameliorate its dark side: regulation, representation and renewal.

Regulation seeks to rein in aspects of corporate behaviour by setting standards for wider benefit, in law or through governance structures. Meeting these standards usually comes at a cost to business, one it might prefer not to pay: in terms of community engagement; environmental protection; or guarantees for redundancy or sick leave, for instance. A voluntary variant is the balanced scorecard, where businesses monitor themselves against social or environmental measures as well as against traditional business goals.

We recognize that regulation alone will not suffice to fill the moral vacuum. Laws, codes of practice or lists of rules may curb poor behaviour, but they cannot make people nicer to, or care more about, each other. Regulation might make companies firmer but not always fairer. That said, business best practice codes are of enormous benefit, as we shall see.

Representation, through unions, workers' councils, non-executive directors and so on, broadens the range of interests that steer a business (and might even be mandated by regulators). As a rule, the more viewpoints that inform strategy and operations, the better. Where those views conflict with each other, however, the business is still at the mercy of whichever wins out. The moral vacuum gets filled with the outcome of each struggle for supremacy.

Finally, *Renewal*. With new waves of technology or new ways of doing things, there have been those who have maintained that enlightened self-interest is sufficient to drive more humane business behaviour. H L Gantt[13] (he of the famous chart) and F W Taylor[14] (father of scientific management), for instance, both advocated getting the best from people by providing rest periods and not overstressing them.

Even Henry Ford had enlightened views. His technical training institution, for instance, paid trainee scholars a bursary and piecework rates for what they produced, while he measured workloads in his factories so that the disabled could deliver and be paid on the same basis as their able-bodied peers. Moreover, he maintained that self-interest, not charity, drove such decisions.

New businesses are spinning out billionaire entrepreneurs and transforming our lives, from our cars to how we consume content. At their worst, some of these companies hit the news for worker exploitation or for manipulating the gig economy; we are uncomfortably aware of a wage-slave underclass that keeps our lifestyles afloat.

At best, however, they produce great jobs, even if they are principally for a creative and well-educated but growing elite. Some are experimenting with remuneration schemes that look to the future as well as to the bonus-eligible last quarter, with relatively low salary ceilings and everything else in stock. Some encourage workers to take whatever holiday they want, and to take plenty of it. Some have policies and practices to promote openness and honesty across the organization and with clients and suppliers. Many lead in environmental sustainability.

Clearly, the leaders of such organizations are trying to do something positive about the moral vacuum.

Working Toward Redemption?

Our contention, as authors, is that these three approaches, however well-meaning and insightful, will either fade with time, or can only achieve a limited impact in cutting back the downside of life in business. Moreover, none have taken a representative hold in the workplace.

Somehow, humanity needs to move behind behaviour itself to the ethics driving it. Value-driven decisions are always trickier to make than decisions based on rules, but that is where we must go next.

In the next chapter, we will present a framework that starts to connect Christian virtue to business excellence. That way, we will begin to identify what the staircase steps of increasing corporate effectiveness and virtue might look like in practice.

Summary

- This chapter presents an explanation of why terrible things happen at work alongside the potential for good.
- This approach also shows why further development of best practice cannot eliminate the darker side of the workplace by itself.

Case Study—Anglo Recycling Technology[15]

This story illustrates intentional Christian management to make a profit and provide meaningful work for the good of employees, the local community and in recycling. This business has maintained its long-term view, adapting to changing situations without altering its publicly promoted core values and has moulded employee behaviour through consistently leading by example. It has survived internal fraud, the 2007–2008 financial crisis, COVID-19 lockdown and ballooning energy prices, episodes during which it has tapped into a well of goodwill built up over a long time. While not describing itself as Christian or kingdom, its behaviour is consistent with a kingdom model.

Lancashire's footwear supply chain before World War II stretched into Germany. In 1938, a Jewish business owner, Hans Neuhaus, abandoned his business exporting pressed hair felt in Speyer because of Nazi reprisals and founded Anglo Felt in Whitworth near Rochdale. Nearly 40 years later, the business had diversified into needlefelts for the carpet and automotive industries, a product made almost entirely from recycled waste. Despite substantial capital investment, the company lost money for years and by 1982 evidence of embezzlement emerged. Peter Riley, a committed Christian and son of the MD of the parent company, agreed to take over to try to avoid its closure. A turbulent period followed for staff, products, suppliers and manufacturing processes. In July 1987, the company was sold to a Yorkshire businessman, Kingston Macaulay, and a year later Kingston's son, Simon, took over. Simon had recently attended an *Alpha* course and had a desire to bring his faith into his work. He approached a local Baptist minister who agreed to regular pastoral visits. Today, all employees sign-up to a (prominently-displayed) Company Charter:

- We commit to tell the truth in all situations at work with colleagues, suppliers and customers. We will behave with integrity in all our business dealings.
- The work we do is valuable and important. We provide jobs for families in the Rossendale Valley. We recycle materials that might otherwise go to landfill. We have a social enterprise that offers work experience for vulnerable adults.
- We are committed to supporting our employees, both in and out of work, as far as we are able. The pastoral support of our company chaplain over the last 10 years is a key commitment for us.
- We want all our staff to play to their strengths. We will endeavour to best tailor each person's job to their own skill set. Everyone has a special gift. We will try and find it.
- We will focus on developing managers that inspire respect and loyalty in their staff, and bring out the best in them.
- All staff need their holidays and a true break from work. We commit to not contact any of our staff on holiday without their prior agreement.
- We commit to investing part of our energy, resources and vision into the community of Whitworth.

For more than 15 years, 10% of the company's profits have been shared equally amongst all staff. Now renamed Anglo Recycling Technology, the business is registering record revenues and profits and every job vacancy attracts huge numbers of applicants, while in 2018 four members of staff celebrated 20 years' service. By working with two local churches it has reopened a popular youth club that the county council could no longer sustain. Ethically and effectively, the business is at the heart of the Whitworth community.

Seeing Business Through a Kingdom Lens

4

> Do you see someone skilled in their work? They will serve before kings.
>
> Prov 22.29
>
> Work hard, have fun, make history.
>
> Jeff Bezos[16]
>
> Work gives you meaning and purpose and life is empty without it.
>
> Stephen Hawking[17]

As authors, we set out to find a way into business decisions that speaks to Christians and to the secular workplace in order to understand what happens when we bring the two together. Here, we propose something simple enough to use quickly, yet sufficiently robust to analyze work-related scenarios.

To work, such a framework must identify a set of core Christian themes and connect them to a set of core business themes. Clearly it helps if there are equal numbers on each side—and there are! The business literature is replete with best practice standards which may be analyzed, while for the Christian side, we cite Paul in 1 Corinthians: 'yet I will show you the most excellent way' (1 Cor 12.31), and 'Now these three remain: faith, hope and love. But the greatest of these is love' (1 Cor 13.13).

Known as the theological virtues, faith, hope and love have fascinated and inspired Christian thinkers from the earliest days. Augustine of Hippo (fourth century AD), for instance, used them as a framework for understanding the gospel, while Thomas Aquinas (thirteenth century AD) connected them to the cardinal virtues of prudence, justice, fortitude and temperance. As authors trying to connect the theological virtues to other aspects of life, we are standing on the shoulders of giants.

The resulting *RR3 Framework*, then, connects the theological virtues to the business-oriented triplet of process, purpose and people on the right as shown here:

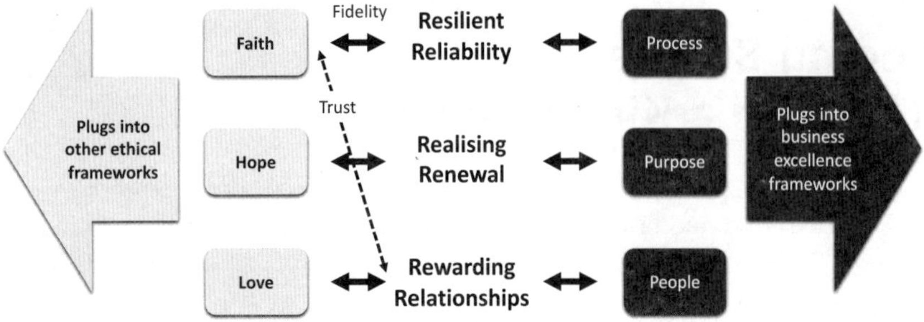

Framework Overview

In what follows we will do three things:

- Summarize best business practice under the themes of *process, purpose* and *people*. Let us call these the business virtues.
- Argue that the theological virtues of faith, hope and love can only be realized in God's strength (Aquinas noted that they flowed directly from God's grace).
- Argue that both the business virtues and theological virtues are surprisingly similar and may be connected through three bridging terms, *resilient reliability, realizing renewal,*and *rewarding relationships*. These connect kingdom values (to the left) to best business (values to the right).

Having done that, a powerful tool emerges to discuss business motivation and practice.

Business Excellence

As authors, we analyzed two widely used business excellence models, the Malcolm Baldrige Award, and the EFQM (European Foundation for Quality Management) Excellence Model, which are used in over 70 countries. The EFQM, for example, believes that at least 30,000 organizations are using its model (the Japanese Deming Prize is probably the next most common approach). While these apply to all sizes of enterprise, the cost and effort of adoption favour uptake by medium and larger-sized companies.

Over the years research has refined their guidance and has begun to reflect more overtly an ethical dimension, for example, in categories such as societal contributions, sustainable development and human rights. EFQM notes that if every company complied, the world would be a better place—something of a kingdom claim.

Prime benefits of such well-attested models are their supporting data and reference material as well as the lenses they offer into business excellence, probing beneath the high-level criteria to provide detailed pictures across and throughout businesses.

It is not difficult to take the criteria in EFQM and Baldrige and reclassify them against purpose, people and process, or to check that everything maps across without leaving gaps in the new taxonomy.[18] Next, the detailed criteria of the excellence models can be used to expand and validate this understanding through the business virtues of purpose, people and process.

Having summarized the right-hand side, the left-hand side of the RR3 framework must now be developed.

Kingdom Excellence

A transparent approach is to view the business virtues as the best anyone can do using their own strength, ingenuity and effort, and the theological virtues as being achievable only in God's strength through grace. Those wishing to bring other ethical positions to bear must still appeal to something higher than themselves to move beyond the business virtues. The bridgehead comes from three connecting terms: resilient reliability, realizing renewal, and rewarding relationships.

Resilient Reliability: Pivoting Around Perfection

Faith leads us to a perfection that we cannot grasp with our own strength. In the gospel it comes as a wonderful surprise and as a gift (Matt 5.48). Meanwhile, business is always counting the cost of imperfection and failure, and its path to success lies in *process*, a combination of technology and procedures. The last 50 years has seen a relentless pursuit of reducing imperfections through extreme standards, such as Six Sigma[19] or Total Quality Management (TQM), together with measures to meet them.[20]

Resilient reliability provides the RR3 Framework's bridge between a gift of perfection to the left and a hard-won journey toward perfection to the right.

This may surprise those expecting Christian businesses to exhibit faith as heroic acts of trust in stakeholders. Process control and faith are both hard-nosed and only useful to the extent that they work! Thus, a virtue that cannot deliver good products is a problem.

Realizing Renewal: Pivoting Around Glory

Christian hope draws us to what we cannot realize in our own strength: the glory of God (hope and glory often go together in the letters of both Paul and Peter).

In our day, Jeff Bezos wants to 'have fun,' but also to make history, while Stephen Hawking saw purpose and meaning in work. The something they are both after is a form of glory—the creative, the end purpose, the capacity to enjoy beauty and renewal. Business puts its hope of glory in purpose, in strategy and in leadership.

Realizing renewal bridges on the left to hope fulfilled in the glory of God, and to the pursuit of ambitious achievements to the right, capturing both aspects of meaning and significance together with an outlet for our creative and organizational urges.

Rewarding Relationships: Pivoting Around the Heart

In many ways, this is the most obvious line in the framework. To the left, it recognizes and responds to God's commitment to love the unlovely, while to the right it highlights the increasing importance of relationships in business.

Business is responding to a growing number of groups whose views must be elicited and whose needs must be satisfied: shareholders, workers, clients, suppliers, subcontractors and external stakeholders.

Rewarding relationships thus connects a Christian calling to love one another on the left with a business focus on people to the right.

What Does This Say to Leaders of Well-run and Profitable Businesses?

These are the businesses in the two lower quadrants of the matrix. Starting with a business that is seeking to achieve maximum profitability and sustainability by adopting business best practices, we note that the call of virtue is usually harder to achieve than any code of practice. Subjecting workers to ever more demanding processes, for instance, may help with quality management, but does not guarantee addressing the ethical challenge on the other side.

Although the RR3 framework brings together concepts that have a degree of similarity, there are important differences. Business practice is governed by guidance and by rules and regulations that need to be documented, communicated and shared. Because business changes with the world around it, ideal practice is constantly being redrafted, reinterpreted and reshared. By contrast, values on the left-hand side remain constant in changing times.

Perhaps Paul was referring to a form of this difference when he talked about the letter killing and the Spirit giving life (2 Cor 3.6). Virtue lives; guidelines start to die as soon as the ink is dry.

All this means that your intangible ethics are anchored in the details of your codes of practice. Following the letter of best practice for the business may do harm elsewhere. Good practice in cash flow management, for example, may mean slowing the payment of invoices to smaller suppliers whose continued business existence can be put at risk as a result.

What Does This Say to the Leader of Any Virtuous Business?

These are the businesses in the top two quadrants of the matrix. The main findings from applying the RR3 Framework to a business that already has an ethical starting point is that the ethical values will be heard most clearly in the business world when they result in recognizably good practice.

There is little point, for instance, in trying to create wealth for a poor community if the company is not viable in the long term or if its practices deliver products of variable quality. There is no point in trying to employ the unemployable unless you have a process to help staff develop their skills (see the case studies on Green Pastures [pp 7–8] and Grace Enterprises [pp 26–27]).

On the other hand, the RR3 Framework provides a language to link Christian hope, for instance, to a wide range of goals for renewal, including greening, community action (see the Anglo Recycling Technology [pp 13–14] case study), or economic and social impact (see the Transcend Support [pp 20–21] case study).

In Conclusion

The RR3 Framework thus supports a dialogue about ethics that can work in either direction. This is often hard to achieve. In extreme cases it may otherwise take a whistle-blower to expose a disconnect between a company's beliefs (or legal duties) and how it operates. By contrast this framework enables a legitimate conversation around why companies behave in contradiction to their intended standards and responsibilities. In the long run, such open dialogues may be the major benefit of this work.

Summary

- The virtues of faith, hope and love can be paired with the business virtues of process, purpose and people to enable a practical dialogue between virtue progressed in God's strength and ethical and operational progress achieved in human strength.

- The resulting framework can be used to give direction to businesses from any starting point in the virtue/kingdom matrix.

Case Study—Transcend Support[21]

This example illustrates an arms-length connection between the Christian virtue of the founders and the operational direction of the business, since the board members do not run the business.

Transcend came out of Jerry Marshall's involvement in Palestine as a consultant. Post Intifada, he felt a fresh call from God to stand with Arab Christians and led a team of entrepreneurs to create employment in an environment where options were highly constrained. A Palestinian Christian working in development, Nassim Nour, was seeking an opportunity to work with such a group, and invited Jerry to facilitate a workshop in 2005 on creating robust jobs that would survive in peace or conflict. The vision that emerged was for a contact centre in Bethlehem, where there are many international schools, and therefore language skills. The team has focused on invisible exports that could not be held up or damaged at the border. Transcend sells bilingual English/Arabic voice services to clients operating across the Middle East and now also offers software development. They started to work with an Israeli company but when that did not work out, they joined up with an American Christian, Russ Sandlin, who had a track record regionally and in the domain. By 2012 they had the funds to launch the business, which grew to 170 staff. The founders do some sales and lead generation but are non-executive directors. The name 'Transcend' connotes several layers of meaning, not just transcending movement restrictions and developing relationships across the political divide and national borders, but also in helping people to rise about daunting circumstances.

At heart, it creates jobs and skills regardless of religion and brings better English and customer care skills to the wider economy (as staff move on). On set-up it was designed to survive even a six-month curfew and so coped well during the pandemic when everyone was able to shift to working from home within two days. Transcend highlights the challenges of retaining a fully Christian ethos over many years. It is known as a Christian-founded company and for the lived-out faith of Christian staff within the company, as well as for modelling integrity and gender equality. More agents are women than men, which needed special arrangements, such as door-to-door transport and often a husband's or father's permission. Moreover, half the senior staff are women. There is no target on faith (staff are approximately 80% Muslim). The first CEO was Christian, while the current CEO is Muslim, although he understands the founders' Christian perspective. Another factor potentially diluting the immediacy of the Christian ethos is the position of the two main investment organizations, which broadly support the impact being achieved but are less committed to its kingdom roots.

Because the founders have chosen to remain at arms' length as non-executives on the board they have traded control for influence, but keep raising the issue of core ethos. Transcend is a wonderful example of creative intervention with a strong kingdom intent. The challenge is managing against the challenge of drift from the kingdom call that launched it.

5 Kingdom Business: Measuring Up

> Campaigns against corporations have led them to take greater care that their goods are not produced under unacceptable working conditions for starvation wages. All of us, by the decisions we make about how we live and work and travel and consume help to shape an environment. To think and act morally, to do what is right because it is right, influences others; it begins to create a climate of opinion; good like evil, is infectious. We do not have to accept the unacceptable. The only thing that makes social or economic trends inevitable is the belief that they are. The unfolding drama of the twenty-first century is one of which we are the co-writers of the script.
>
> Rabbi Jonathan Sacks[22]

For kingdom business, there is no one size fits all, nor a set of measurable criteria to set a boundary above which a claim for a kingdom business ethic may be made. What follows, therefore, is a vision for a direction of travel for business leaders. It is not about achieving every aspect; it is about the incremental steps that keep the business climbing towards the kingdom quadrant in this updated chart.

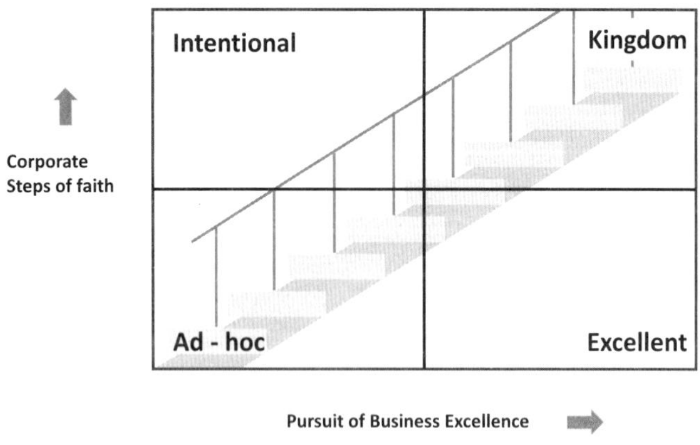

Businesses begin their journey in different places. Selling high-value fashion items to wealthy customers, for example, does not preclude the kingdom ideal nor is a high social impact business is automatically kingdom oriented—each is as it behaves.

Instead of the starting point, let us focus on the destination. As Watts Humphrey said, 'If you don't know where you are a map won't help.'[23] The next section, therefore, presents some methods to find out where you are.

Measuring Up

A proven approach to measuring best practice is the maturity grid. Weak practice is typically *ad hoc* and inconsistent, while strong practice is typically systematic, and also reliable and routinely measured. Maturity grids describe what each type of practice actually looks like on this scale from *ad hoc* to systematic.

To use such a grid, a team from the business would meet with a facilitator to identify which level best describes how the business is running. Views will often vary, since one's department and managerial level affect one's perspective. This approach has already been used with over 10,000 organizations in the international PROBE (Promoting Business Excellence) programme, for example.[24]

As noted, the RR3 Framework can use what is available in terms of business excellence and so PROBE or something similar may be used to position a company along the horizontal axis.

Alongside this booklet, the authors are currently creating a maturity grid to assess a company's ethical position based on the theological virtues. At the time of writing, the tool is under Beta test with volunteer companies and is being called PROVE (Promoting Virtuous Excellence). In this case, the virtue scale runs from 1 (*ad hoc* performance) to 5 (kingdom excellence). Descriptors are provided for levels 1, 3 and 5, allowing teams to interpolate to position themselves as level 2 or 4 as appropriate. Here is an example from this PROVE maturity grid under the *hope* theme, criterion 1 of a set of 23 criteria.

Realizing Renewal (Hope)	**1**	**3**	**5**
1. Business purpose	Whilst the business purpose is essentially expressed in terms of profits and growth, there is an unwritten understanding that business should be a force for good and that unethical behaviours should be called out.	The business purpose goes further than financial goals and firmly embraces social and environmental responsibilities that go beyond simple compliance. The business can hold on to these wider goals during difficult business seasons.	The business purpose is expressed in recognizable kingdom outcomes. Financial sustainability is nonetheless recognized as an essential platform for kingdom outcomes. Kingdom outcomes may both be positive impact (light) and avoidance and correction of negative impact (salt).

Kingdom Business—Purpose Through the Lens of Hope

As described, kingdom outcomes are not just the avoidance and correction of negative impact (salt) but also the achievement of positive impact (light). Note that typical level 3 ethical businesses tend to avoid harm rather than have as an explicit objective to make the world a better place. Note also that businesses increasingly have an opportunity to lead social change that governments cannot achieve.

All businesses must constantly adapt to changing contexts, but for a kingdom business the purpose must remain anchored in a Christian hope of God's glory for the community, the workforce, the customers and even the planet. The trick is to change direction in response to prevailing conditions without changing destination: there must be no creeping secularization of purpose. At the top end, kingdom businesses will seek this through corporate prayer, spiritual partners and retreats.

Kingdom excellence also invites a focus on those products and services which make a positive difference to people's lives and to the sustainability of the planet. Creativity and beauty are to be celebrated—even the abstract elegance of a high-performing supply chain that rewards rather than exhausts the people and resources involved.

That said, there is usually more than one way to view a product. The Anglo-French Concorde airliner, for example, was stunningly beautiful, technologically unique, universally admired and never successfully imitated—a superb example of engineering excellence. However, it became a plaything for the super-rich, consumed inordinate amounts of fuel and was very noisy.

Kingdom Business—People Through the Lens of Love

Here is another example from the PROVE maturity grid:

Rewarding Relationships (Love)	**1**	**3**	**5**
13. Employees	Employees are acknowledged as a key asset of the business and their well-being is important. Employment law, safe working and safeguarding are all taken seriously.	Employee well-being, morale and health are all regularly monitored at an individual level. The approach is one of 'respect for the individual.' Improving personal well-being is a goal of the business.	People are seen not as assets or human resources but as being important in their own right. The business is focused on improving human relationships. People love their jobs and their working relationships.

Many business leaders describe their employees as the company's most important assets while the department responsible for employees is called 'Human Resources.' However, for a kingdom business employees are important in their own right. The business is focused on improving human relationships.

It is tempting to produce a long list of what such an ideal might look like: employees being regularly invited to share their wider life context, caring strongly about the whole person or providing pastoral care (for those of any faith or none at all) might be examples.

More telling, however, is to consider where this makes a radical difference. For instance, a business might aim to develop people's unique abilities to contribute to kingdom purposes rather than profiling them according to what they cannot do.

Kingdom Business—Process Through the Lens of Faith

Finally, one more example from the PROVE maturity grid:

Resilient Reliability (Faith)	**1**	**3**	**5**
20.Process improvement	Opportunities are sought for process improvement in order to reduce costs, improve quality and create better service. The primary drive is top-down. Employee involvement in the identification and realization of these opportunities is not always sought.	All employees, customers and suppliers are actively involved in finding and implementing process improvements. The benefits of better processes are shared with employees, suppliers and customers.	In its single-minded drive for agility and better processes the business remains committed to compassionate execution of all changes with a clear focus on the well-being of employees throughout the supply chain.

What would kingdom excellence in technology acquisition, for example, look like? One might see it as an opportunity to introduce leanness with wholeness by boosting the well-being of employees and the satisfaction of customers and business partners.

In similar vein, environmental sustainability might become a natural part of the kingdom purpose of the business as a deliberate objective (although green washing moves a company further away from any kingdom authenticity).

Postscript

What is the Vision from Here?

As authors, we hope that this book provides tools for thought and for action. First, we have sought to clarify the difference between business best practice and ethical motivation, and to pursue each appropriately and intentionally. Secondly, we presented the RR3 Framework as a way to connect virtuous intentions to the codes of practice by which a business is run. Finally, we have provided a way of developing a framework that connects ethics and practice into an assessment grid that enables you to position your business now and plot its path to kingdom excellence.

Summary

- Maturity grids exist to assess a company's performance along the best practice axis.
- The RR3 Framework can be used in the same way to assess ethical performance of a business.
- The combination of the Staircase matrix, the RR3 Framework and the emerging PROVE maturity grid provide new tools to think about your business and taking it to a more virtuous place.

Case Study—Grace Enterprises

As well as illustrating the importance of combining a Christian drive with sound business practice, and a special emphasis on the rewarding relationships theme, this example shows how a management team has created tools that help staff measure their progress in various dimensions.

After 10 years developing a basic business model and learning by doing, Grace Enterprises was set up in late 2017 by husband-and-wife team Matt (a former teacher) and Sam (a former GP). It is an umbrella charity under which they are building businesses to employ those who have slipped through the societal net. Radiant Cleaners employs 30 people. It was the first business set up under Grace Enterprises and has been running since 2018. Trends in growth are hard to describe because of the pandemic hiatus but, having reported revenues of just over £50,000 for 2017/2018, it was closer to £200,000 by 2022. In a good year, its profit margins are 7–10%. While it still relies on donations, which have varied in its short life from 0% to around 30%, the aim is full sustainability through modest profits without relying on donations. Profits would then be channelled into the next business being launched.

Radiant Cleaners was chosen as the launch business because of the low barriers to entry both in terms of training and up-front investment. The operation involves developing people as far as they can go, since not everyone taken on is capable of a normal workload for the rest of their lives. In 2022, Jubilee Events was launched, which needed more up-front investment (marquee etc), donated by Christians who liked the Radiant Cleaners model. Half the Story was launched in 2023, using yet another business model.[25] All three enjoy the same ethos and offer the same support to those facing serious barriers to work. As well as a sensitive approach to management, Grace Enterprises has created a compass—the *Living Life Index* described below—to help staff identify their progress and plan their development. For some, Radiant Cleaners is a destination employer, while for others it is a stepping-stone to another job. An extreme example of the latter would be a couple from the Pacific Rim who arrived in the UK as refugees with little English, for whom Radiant Cleaners provided a buffer while they found their feet in the UK. One is now employed in aviation while the other may return to the automotive sector in line with their training and background. A more traditional worker might be a substance abuser passing through on the way to full rehabilitation.

To support staff, Sam has created a *Living Life Index*, which is inspired by Jesus' intention that we should live life to the full (John 10.10). This innovation focuses on four key areas: health (mental and physical); home life; work (including transferrable and workplace skills); and personal function and goals, each with categories to explore. Through regular reviews, it supports an intentional dialogue with staff across the whole of their lives and connects progress at work (including wider skills) with development elsewhere. The *Living Life Index* provides a practical and measurable path beyond the people aspects of best business practice and to connect personal development to the performance of the company. As such, it responds to the *rewarding relationships* theme in a creatively Christian manner.

Notes

1 J Welby, *Dethroning Mammon: Making Money Serve Grace* (London: Bloomsbury Continuum, 2016).
2 A G Gardiner, *The Life of George Cadbury* (London: Cassell, 1923).
3 J Collins, *Good to Great* (London: Random House Business Books, 2001).
4 Wikipedia, 'Credo ut intelligam,' 2023 (online). Available at: https://en.wikipedia.org/wiki/Credo_ut_intelligam (accessed 27 July 2023).
5 B Corp Movement, 'Make Business a Force For Good,' 2023 (online). Available at: https://www.bcorporation.net/en-us/ (accessed 27 July 2023).

6 Business in the Community, 'Fairer Greener Together,' 2023 (online). Available at: https://www.bitc.org.uk (accessed 27 July 2023).
7 ASQ, 'What is the Malcolm Baldrige Quality Award?' American Society for Quality, 2023 (online). Available at: https://asq.org/quality-resources/malcolm-baldrige-national-quality-award (accessed 27 July 2023).
8 EFQM, 'Improving Organizations,' 2023 (online). Available at: https://efqm.org (accessed 27 July 2023).
9 Green Pastures, 'A future without homelessness is possible,' Green Pastures CBS, 2023 (online). Available at: https://www.greenpastures.co.uk (accessed 27 July 2023).
10 K J Barnes, *Redeeming Capitalism* (Grand Rapids, MI: Wm B Eerdmans, 2018).
11 A Smith, An Inquiry into the Nature and Causes of the Wealth of Nations (London: W Strahan and T Cadell, 1776).
12 E Chang, *Brotopia: Breaking Up the Boys' Club of Silicon Valley* (New York: Penguin Random House, 2018).
13 H L Gantt, *Organizing for Work* (New York: Harcourt, Brace and Howe, 1917).
14 F W Taylor, *The Principles of Scientific Management* (New York: Harper and Brothers, 1919).
15 Anglo Recycling Technology, 'Anglo Recycling giving textiles a second chance,' *Social Progress*, 2023 (online). Available at: https://www.anglorecycling.com (accessed 27 July 2023).
16 Goodreads, 'Jeff Bezos,' Goodreads, Inc, 2023 (online). Available at: https://www.goodreads.com/quotes/701505-work-hard-have-fun-make-history (accessed 27 July 2023).
17 ABC News, 'The "most important pieces of advice" Stephen Hawking gave to his children,' ABC News, 14 March 2018 (online). Available at: https://abcnews.go.com/International/important-pieces-advice-stephen-hawking-gave-children/story?id=53738211#:~:text=%22Here%20are%20the%20most%20important,life%20is%20empty%20without%20it (accessed 27 July 2023).
18 P Hanson and T Young, 'Great to Goodness,' *Faith in Business Quarterly,* vol 22, no 1, 2022, pp 17-20.
19 The Council for Six Sigma Certification, 'Official Industry Standard for Six Sigma Accreditation,' The Council for Six Sigma Certification, 27 July 2018 (online). Available at: https://www.sixsigmacouncil.org (accessed 27 July 2023).
20 ASQ, 'What is Total Quality Management (TQM),' American Society for Quality, 2023 (online). Available at: https://en.wikipedia.org/wiki/Total_quality_management (accessed 2023 July 2023).
21 Transcend, 'Transcend beyond limits,' Transcend, 2021 (online). Available at: https://www.transcend.ps (accessed 27 July 2023).
22 CSR Company International, 'Memorable words on CSR,' VISION, 2014 (online). Available at: https://www.csr-company.com/resources-corner/words/memorable-quotes-ethics-csr-and-sustainability (accessed 27 July 2023).
23 AZ Quotes, 'If you don't know where you are, a map won't help,' Wind and Fly LTD, 2001-2023 (online). Available at: https://www.azquotes.com/quote/731348 (accessed 27 July 2023).
24 Lean Business Ireland, 'PROBE explained,' Lean Business Ireland (online). Available at: https://www.leanbusinessireland.ie/wp-content/uploads/2018/08/PROBE-explained_v2018-01.pdf (accessed 27 July 2023).
25 *ibid.*